"A man must love a thing very much if he practices it without any hope of fame or money, but even practice it without any hope of doing it well…"

EntreWorshippers

Conversations with Artists,
Entrepreneurs, Business Leaders,
Change Agents, and Risk Takers who
Work by Faith and Impact Culture

Curated by
Brian Sooy

Visit EntreWorship.com for more inspiration and encouragement as you re-examine what it means to work by faith.

Unless otherwise indicated, all Scripture quotations are taken from the Holy Bible, New Living Translation, copyright © 1996, 2004, 2007, 2013, 2015 by Tyndale House Foundation. Used by permission of Tyndale House Publishers, Inc., Carol Stream, Illinois 60188. All rights reserved.

Select passages of Scripture from the GOD'S WORD Translation (GW). Learn more about this easy-to-read translation at godsword.org.

Ebook ISBN: 978-9781508074748
ISBN-13: 978-1546631453
ISBN-10: 1546631453

First Printing 2017

Readers Respond to EntreWorship:

"Brian Sooy cares deeply about entrepreneurs and about Christ. This book shows how the two are so powerfully, and masterfully, intertwined."

— Leslie Bianco | *Author and Founder*
In the Company of Prayer
companyofprayer.com

In an era in which we often worship entrepreneurs, Brian brings believers back to the right perspective on entrepreneurship. We create, because we are children of the Creator. EntreWorship hits the core of the things that many of struggle with in our ventures: isolation, feelings of inadequacy, impatience, busyness and more. This isn't just a read once and toss type of book, but a guide that you need to keep close by and read often!

Todd Greer, PhD | *Chief Catalyst*
The Exchange (A CoWorking Community)
Exchange202.com

"Such a man must love the toils of the work more than any other man can love the rewards of it."

G.K. Chesterton

For those who work and worship:

Keep the faith.

Put your hand to the plow.

Don't look back.

The world needs people like you: entrepreneurs, leaders, disruptors, change agents, and explorers who do not fear the narrow path.

As an entrepreneur who has a living and active relationship with Jesus Christ, I want my work to be full of worship, and to avoid our culture's obsession with the worship of entrepreneurship.

From my perspective, work is worship — but I don't worship work.

I've been thinking a lot about being an entrepreneur, and the believer's role as an entrepreneurial leader. With this perspective in mind, these thoughts and this idea of EntreWorship may not be for you, and that's OK.

I've always believed entrepreneurship is a way of thinking. Entrepreneurship principles are teachable; to be an entrepreneur, you must think like one.

Worship is a way of thinking that can have a profound and deep influence on how we live. When we think first of the One whom we worship, and who he has called us to serve in love, we begin to know God's will for us. It's transformational. To be transformed, you must allow God to change the way you think.

The Apostle Paul challenged the Romans in Chapter 12, 1-2:
> *And so, dear brothers and sisters, I plead with you to give your bodies to God because of all he has done for you. Let them be a living and holy sacrifice — the kind he will find acceptable. This is truly the way to worship him. Don't copy the behavior and customs of this world, but let God transform you into a new person by changing the way you think.*

Then you will learn to know God's will for you, which is good and pleasing and perfect.

I believe our culture, including church culture, has a flawed perspective about work. Business culture celebrates leaders; the church talks about leadership but wants followers.

Entrepreneurs tend to be leaders, and not always good followers.

It's not a fault; it's the way you and I are wired. In the tension in between live those who want to live by faith and do work that matters, following their Lord and leading with the gifts and insights they have been given. We all struggle; we all yearn for success.

There must be more to the journey of faith and lifestyle of entrepreneurship than prosperity; the drive for success needs to drive you to want to profit from your business, or all you're left with is a hobby.

I believe the Bible contains much wisdom that is relevant to entrepreneurs. I also believe that an entrepreneurial perspective on the Bible and faith is needed for today.

The last thing we need is "The Entrepreneur's Bible;" what we need is to have a biblical perspective on entrepreneurship and an entrepreneurial perspective of worship.

The intersection of work and faith is what I call *EntreWorship*. You who work by faith are EntreWorshippers.

Re-imagining Work

A Conversation with Todd Greer

I've been a tenant in a building designed to be a startup incubator, but I've never been a member of an entrepreneurial community like The Exchange 202 in Mobile, Alabama. There's a huge difference — community is organic and requires a human catalyst — a reactive agent a physical space doesn't provide.

At the co-working community The Exchange in Mobile, Alabama, the motto is "Re-imagine Work."

Recognizing that technology empowers anyone to work anywhere they choose, its members choose to work in an environment to have access to people, ideas, and collaborative tools that help them reach new levels. The Exchange's focus centers on cultivating a creative culture where members feel free to engage other thinkers and doers.

Somewhere in that mix is an individual with a title that hints at someone who makes things happen: Chief Catalyst.

After almost two decades of work in nonprofit organizations, building capacity through communications and leadership development, Todd Greer, PhD. (Organizational Leadership, Regent University) recognized a need for a "third space" (not a traditional home or corporate environment) that could facilitate the movement of people, ideas, services, products, and organization.

Todd's mission in life is to grow others through the engagement of their "sweet spot" where they can thrive in teams, organizations and especially as people.

The PhD after Todd's name reveals he's well-educated, smart, and filled with emotional intelligence.

Todd and I have intermittent conversations; some short, some long, on Twitter, via text, sometimes on the phone or video chat. This conversation is no different, taking place between text and email.

I asked Todd how he approaches his work as worship, or as he might suggest, re-imagining work as worship:

> Todd: "Thanks for being such a great source of encouragement and inspiration. I am excited to be part of a community here in Mobile that, for all its faults and shortcomings, is allowing individuals and groups to make real impact for the growth of our community!"

EW: 2 Thessalonians 1:11 reads, "So we keep on praying for you, asking our God to enable you to live a life worthy of his calling. May he give you the power to accomplish all the good things your faith prompts you to do."

EW: Is Exchange 202 a response to a prompting of your faith?

Todd: "The Exchange was a response to a need in my own life for developing a connected community. Having spent almost a decade in full-time ministry, but feeling a deep desire for a community that fit into the third space realm (not traditional home or work), I worked with some great co-founders and partners to be able to shape a space that is welcome and inviting to all (much like the spiritual community should be)."

"I have long looked for a way to help others in their developmental processes and the Exchange allows me to cheer them on, build them up, and connect them for deeper growth."

2 Thessalonians continues: (1:12) Then the name of our Lord Jesus will be honored because of the way you live, and you will be honored along with him."

EW: You are an encourager and quick to call attention to the success of others, without drawing attention to yourself. How do you think this brings honor to Jesus?

Todd: "The truth is, community is at the very core of what I believe we are called to embody as the people of God. In Romans 12:10, the Apostle Paul calls the body to "Love one another with brotherly affection. Outdo one another in showing honor." (ESV)"

"I believe there is so much that happens each day that gets lost in the distractions and noise of this world. We want to be champions for positive growth in the lives of our members and our community."

"It isn't always easy to say, "It's not about me," but I think the more that we can be on the frontlines as encouragers for others we ultimately find our own strength is not in ourselves but in Christ and ALL creation"

The Exchange 202 web site reads "Do what you love. Love where you do it."

EW: How do you do your work and serve the Exchange community with love?

Todd: "I jokingly share that on any given day I play a wide variety of roles. The idea of being a catalyst is about helping things move in the right direction. Because I love my community and our members, I want them to experience excellence in all that we do."

"Sometimes that means helping them find connections that can help them move their work, other times it includes providing new opportunities for learning or new resources, and sometimes it just simply means being available to listen."

Todd: "Paul talks about the importance of shining like stars (Philippians 2:15), Jesus says that we are to be a light set on a hill (Matt. 5:14). Personally, and with the entire Exchange experience, want to be a beacon that welcomes all people to come together to share in life together — regardless of background, beliefs, race, etc."

"Every day I learn something new that reveals to me what love, community, and grace looks like."

"Every day, I know I fall far short of being all that Christ has called me to be, but I want to use all that I can to bring honor and that includes simply giving a community that can help them thrive in their work and as people."

"Do what you love.

Love where you do it."

Peace, Love, and Barbecue

A Conversation with John Rivers

In the south, barbecue is as common as take-out pizza in a college town. 4 Rivers Smokehouse is different — the barbecue is delicious; what makes it different is its mission and the man who founded it as his "barbecue ministry" in 2004, when he hosted a cookout fundraiser to support a local family whose young daughter was battling cancer.

John says, "This was never supposed to be a restaurant. My definition of helping meant doing what felt most natural when comfort was in order — feed those in need."

I sat down with John Rivers for a conversation about working with faith and the greater purpose behind what he does. We talked about how their faith makes a difference to his work and the calling behind his career.

We met in John's office in Winter Park, Florida, where John sat in a recliner, (feet up), and sipped a cup of coffee.

John is soft-spoken. The windows were open; at times the commuter rail line filled the room with the sound of steel wheels on rails and the rumble of diesel engines.

EntreWorship: How critical is faith in Christ to your journey as an entrepreneur?

John: "Quite honestly, you almost pity the entrepreneur who doesn't (have faith in Christ) because there's so much risk that's involved. There's so much unknown. I think it would be very had to go about it without having the faith element. If it were easy (being an entrepreneur), everybody would be doing it."

On entrepreneurship: "It's like you're walking into a buzzsaw on purpose because there's a reward on the other side of it. I think it's when you start getting into it and you take those steps, that's when you find out why so few people are doing it."

EW: Why is faith so important to you as an entrepreneur?

John: "Faith is important when the tough times come. I miss those days to a degree because that was the time when we had many perils, and we didn't know how to fix it."

"We didn't know the answers. At one point we were literally down to 60 days of cash between my wife and I before we opened. That was the time I was closer to God than I ever had been in my whole life. It reminds me of that old saying that 'sometimes it takes getting to a point where all you have is Jesus until you realize all you need is Jesus.'

Joking aside, I think there's a reason for that."

EW: What did those early days when you were closest to God teach you?

John: "I think God brings you there because he's preparing you. He'll give you all this greatness but says, 'I have to teach you first. It's through Me, and it's by Me, and quite frankly, you're only going to get there with Me.'"

"The story that I share with people is about when David was anointed to be king. People don't realize it was 12 years later that he was called to be the king. It was during those 12 years he was in the desert running for his life."

"Bill Johnson wrote an excellent book about it, and he talks about how God uses those turmoil times in our lives to strengthen our relationship with Him. When you do face other challenges later, then you know that you're going be able to turn to Him — it's called strengthening yourself in the Lord. Absent of that turmoil time, you would never have developed the strength and perseverance that's necessary."

EW: I recall the story of Uzziah in 2 Chronicles 26 and its two key lessons. First, as long as Uzziah sought the Lord's guidance, the Lord gave him success in everything he did. God enabled him to build a massive army and reign for 52 years.

Second, at the end of his life, he burned incense in the temple, and 80 priests came in and confronted him. "What are you doing? Burning incense is the work of the priests!" they said. Josiah became outraged with them for their rebuke. The Lord made him prosperous; he became strong; he became powerful — yet his pride brought him down.

At that point when the priests charged in, that's where it says, "He broke out with a skin disease, like leprosy or something, and they rushed him out of there. He spent the remainder of his days ruling in exile, basically in a house across grounds from his palace. His son took care of the day-to-day work of the kingdom.

EW: Do you fight with pride?

John: "Pride is a terrible sin. Oh, yes, especially in the early years. Success is a double-edged sword, especially in a new endeavor when you pour your heart and soul into it. It's just like when you have a child; you're very proud. The more successful that child becomes, comes the pride with it. Hence the challenges, and trying to talk about how God prepares you for challenges later. It wasn't business or financial. It was the tests of my heart, soul, pride."

"With success comes temptations, and with success also comes laziness. There's a lot of things with which you wrestle. And I'm convinced that with getting the business started are a unique set of challenges, but it's the latter ones that you get when you're successful that are greater personal challenges to you."

EW: Do you have a board of directors that help you?

John: "I've got a group of advisors, and most of them are also investors in our business, but not all of them — from former restaurateurs to legal, to accounting, to pastors."

"I'll bring them together maybe once a year. I'll tap into each one as the need arises, to respect their time as well. They've been wonderful throughout the years."

The Unexpected Call(ing)

In 2004, John Rivers received a phone call that changed the course of his life and led to his calling.

John: "It was a mistaken call that came into my private line. Here we are 13 years later, and we still don't know who the phone call came from. It wasn't a mistaken call because the words that they used were, "Mr. Rivers, Mr. Rivers, I'm so sorry about to hear about your daughter."

EW: In your "I Am Second" video, you share about that call that you received.
John: "Yeah — I just don't know where that call came from. What's not on that video is that the phone call came through my private line. There were only two or three people who knew that phone number."

EW: In Ephesians, the Apostle Paul talks about doing works that God prepared for us beforehand, and I noticed this passage a few weeks ago in 2 Thessalonians:

Paul writes, "We keep on praying for you, asking God to enable you to live a life worthy of His calling. May He give you the power to accomplish all the good things your faith prompts you to do."

I'm always wrestling with this tension: Theologians and pastors teach us, "God's got a plan for your life. He's called you to do these things, seeking His will."

At the same time, this verse suggests we have some freedom. We can respond with our heart, and act to do something prompted by our faith.

EW: Was 4 Rivers Smokehouse a response to what your faith prompted you to do, or was it just a response to that situation?

John: You know, that's sometimes the beauty of it. I think people would love it to be cut and dry, "Okay, God is asking me to do this." The word "heart" is used several hundred times in the Bible. It's third only to "God" and "Lord." And people often speak about clarity, and quite frankly, part of clarity is they want control. You know, "'Tell me what's going to happen so that I know that you're there.'"

Faith is not the provision of insight and future and control; faith is being able to walk in the absence of insight, knowledge of the future, and control.

"Faith is not the provision of insight and future and control; faith is being able to walk in the absence of insight, knowledge of the future, and control. People confuse the difference between the two. When you get that prompt on your heart, that's where the faith comes in to be able to discern, 'Okay, is this truly what God is stirring me to do?' I always contend that it's one thing to pray to ask God what He wants you to be doing. It's another thing when He tells you what it is. You have to have the courage to do it."

"So many people say, 'I'm not sure that's what He wants me to be doing,' because that's too big of a change or too big of a risk."

"Was it a movement in faith? Was it faith that moved me? What I would say is that whether I wanted it or not, it was faith that got me through it. Like I said, with the perils that we faced, my gratitude is high today because those perils (of the early business) are what galvanized us as a team — not just the people that are here — but God being a part of that team. Some of the things that happened were far beyond our capability."

EW: What are some circumstances where you experienced God's influence and activity in your young business? Your story reminds me of Ephesians 3:20, where the Apostle Paul prays "Now all glory to God, who is able, through his mighty power at work within us, to accomplish infinitely more than we can ask or think."

John: "There had been so many things! In the early days were struggling back in the garage on how to do catering, how to deliver it hot. I was looking at every van and truck that went by, and my wife finally said, 'Would you stop testing this and just pray?'"

"And I did (pray), and this is a true story: That Monday, Jeff (who's my business partner) and I were up in Daytona, and on the way back to Winter Park I received a phone call from a complete stranger whose kids go to the same school as mine. He buys cars at auctions and sells them. He says, "I bought this lot of cars and it's got this catering truck in it. I didn't know what to do with it so I parked it in your driveway.""

"When I came home Monday the answer to the prayer was in my driveway. He says, 'Whatever you want to pay me is fine.' There are so many stories that are like that."

"But to me, I love it because it's God continuously showing up and reminding me. Every time we've needed a key person or a key position filled, it's just utterly amazing how God just walks that person in the front door."

"Throughout the last seven years, people ask, 'How are you going to raise this money?' or, 'How are you going to open up?'"

"It's a dependency, a faith that God will show up. It drives my CFO crazy... but He does, every time."

EW: One of my marketing agency's core principles is clarity. Do you spend time as a team in prayer as part of your day-to-day business?

John: "What we do is voluntary every morning at 9:30am. We like to start the day just with a short verse and just a brief prayer time. Different people show up on different days, based on the season in their life."

"My immediate team and I do constant book studies. Every Monday we all convene after we have read another chapter in the book. Right now, we're reading "Love Works" by Joel Manby, it's a beautiful book about treating people with love and respect from a managerial perspective, and we take it apart for an hour every Monday as a team."

"It will be a different book five weeks from now, and they're always faith-based books. That's a nice way to keep our focus together as a team. It's not a Bible study. It's taking the book's principles, translating them and applying them in our day-to-day practices as a management team. The theory is if we live it first, everybody else in the company will follow."

EW: So how would you define clarity?
John: I think clarity comes on the backside of the decision process, not the front side. I think that's a big misunderstanding. I think once you've gone through whatever a question is and thought about it, prayed about it, I think clarity comes once you get to that point that you feel confident that this is the right decision, 'This is what God wants me to be doing. This is the direction I'm going to go.'

"There's still peace in it. Truett Cathy told me, 'Don't write a business plan.'"

"Coming out of Johnson & Johnson, I said, "What do you mean don't write a business plan? Why not?""

"Truett says, "Because then you gotta stick to it." The point that he was making is to your question of clarity: set yourself to a purpose and let God work out the details of how you get there and how you achieve it. When we have a side blinders on, we don't see the other opportunities that God has really placed in front of us that get us there and perhaps we end on an unconventional path."

I've got a saying that I keep telling the team that, "If you're not sure of the right decision and you're not forced to make that decision right now, don't force yourself to make the decision."

"So many people get so caught up in the anxiety of the unknown, of not being sure of that right decision, they rush it. Another saying of mine is, "Make up your mind. You're either going to walk on the left side of the road or the right side. When you stand in the middle of the road, that's when you're hit by a truck."

"That process of deciding which side can make myself and people crazy. By being patient with it and waiting, eventually you feel and you hear it. I recall Max Lucado saying that the understanding of the Greek translation of the word "patient" is very different from our understanding of the word patient. The Hebrew interpretation and the Greek interpretation means to be in preparation. It doesn't mean to be waiting on your laurels. It's about God preparing you for when that point of clarity comes. When your heart and your mind and your soul and your spirit aligned to it, you're ready to go."

The Big Leap Into the Entrepreneur Life

A Conversation with Megan Constantino

Megan and Frank Constantino formed Parachute Partners in 2016 as a public relations and business acceleration firm.

Megan's motto, "We Jump With You," means that when you make that jump, she's willing to jump with you.

Megan shared her perspective on how she serves her clients with love:

2 Thessalonians 1:11 reads, "So we keep on praying for you, asking our God to enable you to live a life worthy of his calling. May he give you the power to accomplish all the good things your faith prompts you to do."

EntreWorship: How is Parachute Partners a response to a prompting of your faith and calling?

Megan: "God made me a talker and encourager. What I do is connect amazing people to journalists all day. I talk. That encourages them. The media coverage encourages them. I had the desire of running my own firm in my early twenties but didn't see it feasible. I didn't realize that with time and ample support from a future network, I would receive that. The way to Parachute Partners was paved for years, one relationship at a time. Bigger than landing headlines, we transparently share with clients our reliance and joy in the Lord. So, perhaps it is a side door ministry?"

2 Thessalonians continues: (1:12) Then the name of our Lord Jesus will be honored because of the way you live, and you will be honored along with him."

EW: You are one of the most positive people I know. You give selflessly, without drawing attention to yourself. How do you think this brings honor to Jesus?

Megan: "Wow, what a compliment! I just try to treat people right. I try to bless them. I know that the Lord wants us to operate from a place of love. Generosity is a choice that a believer never regrets. This is true with your time, energy, and resources."

EW: How do you serve your clients (and others) with love?

Megan: Their success is my measure of success in my work but they are family. When you love someone, you think about them. This doesn't occur just during work hours;

you are always looking out for them. I can't turn on the television or open a newspaper without thinking, "How can we leverage this for our clients?" Or, "How can our clients help in this situation?"

EW: How do you approach your work as worship, and how are your business endeavors an expression of worship for you?
Megan: "My work is an exercise of faith. It takes faith to do bold things. I recognize that the success comes from Him. Our story is His story and that doesn't mean outside of the 9 to 5 realm. He is there all day wanting us to allow him to join us in our work."

Generosity is a choice that a believer never regrets. This is true with your time, energy, and resources."

We discussed one last thought on why Megan wanted to share her story:

Megan told me, "I would love to share my story because it's a mess that folks may find helpful," and she had a thoughtful reply to my comment: "We are all beautiful disasters, living in crooked houses built with scarred hands, held together with nails of grace."

EW: Why is your story a mess?

> Megan: "My story is a mess because often I rely on me and not HIM. I am a doer, a fixer, Type A. I end up working too much and out of balance with family. I need to be more Type J as in Type Jesus. Self-reliance in the good, bad, ugly, or beautiful will eventually lead to a mess. He died for me, my sins, aka my mess. I am only clean by His blood."

We are indeed beautiful disasters, redeemed by blood, working to worship the One who gave us the gifts of life and work.

Let's help each other keep the mess to a minimum.

"I need to be more Type J as in Type Jesus."

Entrepreneurship culture is enamored with fast growth. Do you dive in, wade in — or running fast and fearlessly take a wild leap of faith into the arms of the God who cares?

Think back on your entrepreneur journey. Did the stages of your business growth look like these?

- **Stage One: The Great Idea** — (aka "What was I thinking?' after a year or so).
- **Stage Two: The Bungie Cord Jump** — At this stage, you've made the jump into running your business, but you're not certain your cord is short enough until you reach the end of the jump.
- **Stage Three: The Treadmill** — This stage can last several years, while you maintain the momentum you've built in a steady manner. Not too fast, not too slow. It's just like running a marathon: plan for the long haul at the pace you are most comfortable with.
- **Stage Four: Juggling** — Managing projects as a juggler would manage multiple balls: Several must be high enough in the air to give you time to juggle three or four right in front of you.
- **Stage Five: Plate Spinning** — Once you've got the firm running well, with staff to enable you to manage more projects, you move into the role of manager and business developer, keeping all the plates spinning on the sticks. This stage is inseparable from Stage Three. It can also look like the Juggling Stage.

We are all beautiful disasters,

living in crooked houses

built with scarred hands,

held together with nails of grace.

–Brian Sooy

Transcending Time and Anchoring Culture

A Conversation with Makoto Fujimura

The highest calling of an artist who follows Christ is to "truth and beauty," following the admonition from Philippians 4:8:

> *"And now, dear brothers and sisters, one final thing.*
> *Fix your thoughts on what is true, and honorable, and right,*
> *and pure, and lovely, and admirable. Think about things that*
> *are excellent and worthy of praise."*

From Culture Care to the Golden Sea and The Four Holy Gospels, Makoto Fujimura's body of work transcends time and anchors culture. Add faith and grace to truth and beauty, and his work embodies that which makes art, life, and faith full of richness and meaning.

I was introduced to Makoto by my colleagues and fellow members of CIVA (Christians in the Visual Arts), and

31

personally at a CIVA conference in Montreal many years ago. For Makoto, the introduction may not have been memorable; for me, it opened my eyes and mind to a Christ follower who makes a cultural and societal impact through his work, calling, and faith.

As I observe the creative and cultural awareness of modern Christianity, it is regrettable that Makoto's work and influence are not familiar to most of the faithful. Yet his work influences modern culture despite our collective ignorance.

As a collector of original fine art, I supported the retrospective monograph of his career, "Golden Sea" through Kickstarter — knowing that while I may never be able to own one of his original works — I may come to understand his thinking and approach to art.

Busy with his role at the Brehm Center and his collaboration with Martin Scorcese on "Silence," (the film based on Shusako Endo's 1966 book, Silence), Makoto offered his thoughts on how his faith prompts him to work and worship.

This conversation will refer to him as "Fujimura," as he is known to his fans and followers.

2 Thessalonians 1:11 reads, "So we keep on praying for you, asking our God to enable you to live a life worthy of his calling. May he give you the power to accomplish all the good things your faith prompts you to do."

EW: How are your creative work, your writing, and your International Arts Movement a response to a prompting of your faith?

Fujimura: "All I endeavor to do is part of my faith action, to see every day as immersed in my journey with Christ."

2 Thessalonians continues: (1:12) Then the name of our Lord Jesus will be honored because of the way you live, and you will be honored along with him."

Q: As time goes by, how has your perspective on culture care evolved? How do you think this brings honor to Jesus?

Fujimura: "God will be the final judge and I would not dare guess on what I feel on my side is limited. Culture Care has been a long journey even as far back as my childhood in Japan. It has been sharpened by the need for such a mediated language during the intense Culture Wars reality we have now come to inhabit."

"So many influences including my family, my relationships, and theological import has shaped Culture Care thinking. I am developing a thesis for Theology of Making (my next book) that undergirds Culture Care as well."

EW: What are you most passionate about, and how does that find expression at the intersection of your work and worship?

Fujimura: "I have recently completed a cycle of liturgical paintings at my church in Princeton (All Saints) and I am deeply grateful for their willingness to do those works.

I am also grateful for the new Museum of the Bible to house the original Four Holy Gospels paintings to create a chapel around it as part of the inaugural exhibit there opening in November 2017."

EW: How are your work and creativity an act of serving with love? Do you ever consider it to be "rebellious for good" in any way?

Fujimura: "I have used an expression "transgress in love," — not to sin — but to transgress beyond tribal norms to express borderlands language. All creative acts are flowing out of the gratuitous love of God."

EW: How do you personally approach your work as worship, and how are your work and creativity an expression of worship?

Fujimura: "I consider my life and my art to be an offering to worship our Living God. There are many time I fall short. I get back up every day to ask God to fill me with the Holy Spirit (the generative source of all creativity) to create, to love, and to breathe."

Questions to Answer:

Why should your work and entrepreneurial endeavors include the dimension of truth and beauty? How will work as a creative act make your work and life more meaningful?

Think about the art of business and the business of art. Don't settle for bad design in business or within the church; for a one-dimensional experience of worship that centers on 20 minutes of song on Sunday morning, or live with a disconnect between your faith (theology) and work (the practice of your faith).

Embrace work as worship in its fullness. Within the body of Christ, your gifts are given to build the body (the Church), not only for you to earn a living. If the corporate or denominational expression of the Church doesn't understand or allow you to share your talents or skills, the business expression of the Church does and wants you to.

You're a valued member of the faith economy.

When you find a way to serve with your God-given gifts through your business (or art, or as an entrepreneur), you'll find your calling, and you'll begin to understand the value of work as worship. As Francis Schaeffer reminds us, "Christ redeemed the whole person," not just the spiritual part.

It's time to be made whole, in your thinking and your work.

Visit entreworship.com for suggested reading.

Ambassadors, Marketers, and Vessels

A Conversation with Dr. Shelette Stewart

The beauty of being connected by faith is the unanticipated connection God makes between us when least expected. God's providence makes it clear there are no chance meetings, which is how I met consultant and author Dr. Shelette Stewart.

With over 20 years of leadership experience in Fortune 500 companies including The Coca-Cola Company, Dr. Stewart is the founder and principal of Stewart Consulting, LLC, a business consulting and leadership development firm.

She oversees strategic partnerships with global corporations for Harvard Business School, is a Fulbright Foreign Scholarship Program Specialist, and holds a Doctorate in Business Administration and is the author of "Revelations in Business: Connecting Your Business Plan with God's Purpose and Plan for Your Life."

I asked Dr. Stewart how she approaches her work as worship — or as she suggests — connects her profession with her purpose and calling:

2 Thessalonians 1:11 reads, "So we keep on praying for you, asking our God to enable you to live a life worthy of his calling. May he give you the power to accomplish all the good things your faith prompts you to do."

EntreWorship: In what way has your calling and business career been a response to a prompting of your faith?

Dr. Stewart: "My faith has been a consistent thread in my career. When I look back at some of the most critical decisions I've had to make in business — particularly as an entrepreneur — my faith was crucial."

"When God called me out of corporate America, where I was serving in a leadership role for The Coca-Cola Company to start my business and write my book, "Revelations in Business," it was one of the more horrendous times in our country from an economic perspective. It was during the years of 2007 to 2009, and it was truly His promptings and my faith that sustained me."

2 Thessalonians continues: (1:12) Then the name of our Lord Jesus will be honored because of the way you live, and you will be honored along with him.

EW: You're a leadership and business consultant. How does your work with leaders and corporations bring honor to Jesus?

Dr. Stewart: "I believe that the best way for us to bring

honor to Jesus in our work is for us to exemplify Him in the workplace and marketplace. We're His ambassadors. We're marketers for Him. So, from a practical standpoint, this means doing my best to embody the fruit of the Spirit: love, peace, joy, kindness, etc., when working with colleagues and clients. It also means being a person of character, keeping my word, and making sure that my work exemplifies excellence because we serve a God of excellence."

EW: You write "We don't have a personal life and a professional life; we have ONE life and we have to make that life count!" — How does this one assertion serve as the anchor of your writing and practice?

"Dr. Stewart: This belief informs the way I live my entire life. I write about it and practice it because I truly believe it. Our life is not a dress rehearsal. This is the real deal. You know in the Western world, and particularly in the United States, we spend more time at work than we do with our loved ones. Our careers consume over half of our lives."

"We've all have heard the reports from Harvard and other leading researchers reporting that in some cases, 70% of American workers are dissatisfied with their jobs or careers."

"This hurts my heart, especially when we are blessed to have so many options in the U.S. I always say, we spend too much time at work not to enjoy it. I believe it's imperative that what we spend most of our waking hours doing, for most of our lives, is also spiritually edifying."

EW: How do you personally approach your work as worship, and how are your business endeavors an expression of worship?
Dr. Stewart:"I believe that business is a form of ministry and that our work should be a blessing. My pastor relayed this notion in a recent sermon when he reminded us that God blessed Adam and Eve with jobs and work managing the Garden of Eden before they sinned, before the downfall."

"Work is meant to be a blessing. Work is not the result of a fallen world. This truth helps me keep worship in the proper perspective. I am thankful to God and worship Him for allowing me to serve as one of His vessels in the marketplace. I travel the world speaking on purpose-driven leadership, and the topic that I'm most requested to speak on is connecting your profession with your purpose, and your career with your calling."

"This connection and alignment are what I strive for. It's worship. It's a way of giving glory to God by making sure that all I do aligns with His plan and His agenda."

EW: What advice would you give to an entrepreneur or business leader who wants their faith to make their work more

meaningful?

Dr. Stewart: "The first step is to begin from within. Pray and ask the God who created us, and who resides in all of us, what His purpose is for you. Pray, meditate, and contemplate your calling as an individual. We serve a loving God. He's not going to give us a purpose and not tell us what it is. It's up to us to be intentional and diligent in asking."

"Once you have a better idea of your purpose, the key is to connect every aspect of your business plan to His plan and purpose for your life. This is what my book is about: I've learned that His Word must always serve as the spiritual foundation for my professional and commercial endeavors."

Embracing Beauty

A Conversation with Ned Bustard

If your circles of influence intersect with an artist or designer, I encourage you to spend as much time with them as their schedule allows.

If that creative individual is a reader and reflects deeply upon their relationship with Jesus Christ, you will have found someone who will challenge your thinking and show you a way to look the world, your work, and faith through the lenses of beauty and truth.

Ned Bustard is a friend, colleague, and co–conspirator in the movement to bring truth to life through design and beauty.

As a designer and illustrator, he draws from story to bring life to images and reveals images that bring stories to life. His work surprises and delights, whether it's to convey truth or bring a smile to the face of a child.

He's collaborative and inventive, building upon collaborations to expand ideas. Ned brought Luckey Haskins to life for my first children's book, and we've collaborated on projects for CIVA (Christian in the Visual Arts, civa.com) and Aespire (aespire.com).

Ned would say, "I'd like to meet the guy you just described."

Witty and graciously self-deprecating, consider this response to his calling: "As I grew in my understanding of the scope of the Bible's teaching on vocation, I saw my calling as a graphic designer as a way to bring glory to God."

EntreWorship: 2 Thessalonians 1:11 reads, " So we keep on praying for you, asking our God to enable you to live a life worthy of his calling. May he give you the power to accomplish all the good things your faith prompts you to do."

How is your creative work, Square Halo Gallery, Worlds End — (The Bustard Empire) a response to a prompting of your faith? Exactly how big is the Bustard Empire?

NEd: "The "Bustard Empire" (as you hilariously call it) feels like it is a mile wide and an inch deep. I do a bunch of things, and some of them are even profitable! My day job is as a graphic designer for World's End Images and Christians in the Visual Arts (CIVA)."

"I am also, at various times, a children's book illustrator, author, and a printmaker. Some of the books I've written, illustrated, or edited include It Was Good: Making Art to the Glory of God, Squalls Before War: His

Majesty's Schooner Sultana, The Chronicles of Narnia Comprehension Guide, Bede's History of ME, History of Art: Creation to Contemporary, The Reformation ABC's, and Bigger on the Inside: Christianity and Doctor Who."

"I'm also the creative director for Square Halo Books, Inc., curator of the Square Halo Gallery, and I serve on the boards of the Association of Scholars of Christianity in the History of Art (ASCHA) and The Row House, Inc. I am a ruling elder in a church I helped plant called Wheatland, and I plan the worship services for our congregation there each week."

Who are you created to be? What were you created to do? Do you relentlessly and freely pursue your calling with the talents and gifts you have been given?

"These pursuits are prompted by my faith in Jesus Christ. When I was younger, I accepted the muddled theology that said there was spiritual work and unspiritual work — I could be a pastor or I could do a pagan job."

"Thankfully, I didn't stay at that spot. Michael S. Horton wrote in Where in the World is the Church? A Christian View of Culture and Your Role in It, "The Reformation freed Christian men and women to pursue their divinely appointed callings in the world with dignity and respect, without having to justify the usefulness of those callings to the church or its missionary enterprise." As I grew in my understanding of the whole scope of the Bible's teaching on vocation, I saw my calling as a graphic designer as a way to bring glory to God."

2 Thessalonians continues: (1:12) Then the name of our Lord Jesus will be honored because of the way you live, and you will be honored along with him."

EW: You're prolifically creative (is that even a phrase?) and often depict ideas and images that may make people uncomfortable or force them to see things differently. How do you think this brings honor to Jesus?

Ned: "I don't set out to make people uncomfortable, but I know that I must. One of my clients will often say with a laugh, "Can you make this design a little less NEDgy?" I did intentionally push the envelope when I created Revealed: A Storybook Bible for Grown-Ups. But I feel like I had a good reason for my controversial curatorial choices. Our society is too comfortable with what we think the Bible says. Or we dismiss it as arcane and irrelevant."

"I want people to take the Bible seriously, and see that it speaks to every facet of human experience. So when I curated and edited that project I looked for all of the scripture passages that are avoided in pleasant conversation, and had all the best printmakers I know take a stab at illustrating them. "Seeing is the starting point!" as my art historian friend Linda Stratford has remarked. I want people to see the glorious Truth in the Bible, and in the world around them. I want Goodness drawn in "large and startling figures," as Flannery O'Connor said. And I work toward embracing Beauty in all its various shapes and sizes."

"As to how all this would bring honor to Jesus, I think a train honors its designer by traveling fast on train tracks. I was designed to make and be creative in a way to reflect my Maker and demonstrate His goodness to the world — whether that goodness is politically correct or not. I may not always be an artist or author or whatnot, but I will always be reflecting some aspect of Jesus since that is God's intent for his adopted kids."

"In the Westminster Shorter Catechism it says that Christ had three offices or jobs — Prophet, Priest, and King ("Christ, as our Redeemer, executeth the offices of a prophet [Deuteronomy 18:15], of a priest [Psalm 11:4], and of a king [Psalm 2:6], both in his estate of humiliation and exaltation."). Although I've seen myself used in the church in all three ways, I think most of my gifts lie in the category of prophet."

"As a prophet (and a very minor one at that!) I want my work to reach people whose "eyes they have closed" and communicate the Truth in a Good and Beautiful way, so that it can eventually be said of them, "blessed are your eyes, for they see, and your ears, for they hear." In that way, I hope I can model the Prophet-Christ, and so bring him honor."

EW: Ned, you're a "maker." I think you and I are much alike, obsessively creative. What are you most passionate about, and how does that find expression at the intersection of your work and worship?

Ned: "I was made to be a maker. It is often hard to imagine how God is going to display his sovereign plan in your life, but looking back now over the last several decades, I can see how his calling to me to be a maker was worked out in his providential care. I have been shaped by the "coincidental" setbacks and opportunities he has given to me. I have had so many things simply laid in my lap that I would never have been able to orchestrate. And the curious projects and people in my life have molded me into an artist I both could not have imagined I would be, and one whose experiences I would have never have dreamed could have been possible in my lifetime.

"As to being "obsessively creative," I don't think of myself that way, but I can report that on numerous occasions my wife has asked me to stop coming up with ideas for a little while. Unfortunately, I've been unable to fulfill that request, but I have stopped spewing out ideas over the dinner table for a few days at a stretch to give her a break. N.T. Wright said, "Those who follow Jesus ought not only to be celebrating [beauty in the world] but contributing to it." And that is what I want to do. "I want to add to the Beauty," as Sara Groves has sung."

As to what I'm passionate about? I'm not sure. Things that fill my mind often include my wife Leslie, printmaking, books, art, music, sailing, leprechauns, my daughters, mermaids, theology, logo design, Narnia, church, CIVA, Ireland, chocolate, old English libraries (preferably with hidden doors), my gallery, and how much the government is going to gouge me in taxes. Somewhere in that wunderkammer of a list are sure to be some of my passions. I picture the intersection of my work and worship like a complex page in the Book of Kells. It is lovely, and interesting, and orderly in its way, but difficult to unravel.

. . . .

EntreWorship Insight:

Birds bring glory to God when they

fly as high (gravity) and as free

as their wings allow (grace).

. . . .

Certain words tend to float up to the surface at that crossing which I find fire my imagination: Glory, Making, Beauty, Faith, and Good. I wrote the essay on Good in my book It Was Good: Making Art to the Glory of God (because the artist Ed Knippers told me to) and it was providential — the idea of "Good" now drives me. While growing up I stubbornly resisted picking a "life verse" as those around me piously did, but when pressed I would say "Test everything. Hold on to the good." (1 Thess. 5:21).

Now I often will quote an excerpt from Exodus 28:2 — "for Glory and for Beauty." That phrase resonates in me deeply. The ideas of Making and Beauty I have already touched on above, but are also captured in the motto I developed for our homeschool: "Forma et Fides" (which is Latin for "Beauty & Faith").

EW: How do you personally approach your work as worship, and how is your work creativity an expression of that approach?

Ned: "There is no dichotomy between my work and my worship. They are all one. Horton again writes: "The Reformation emphasized the truth that God had become human, bringing dignity to earthly, secular life... One need not 'sanctify' art by demanding that it serve the religious or moral interests of the church. Creation is a legitimate sphere in its own right."

"On my website I say that I want to create a place where 'collaboration and imagination intersect, art and faith greet as friends, and good ideas take root and flourish.'"

"That is my desire for my work life, but I also imagine that could be part of a mission statement for a young church to describe what kind of atmosphere they want to create for their times of worshiping God. I have no categories in my life where work ends and worship begins or where creativity stops to allow faith to start. It is all one in my heart and mind. "It will be a great comfort in a dying hour, to think we have glorified God in our lives. It was Christ's comfort before his death: John 17:3, 'I have glorified thee on the earth.'" wrote Thomas Watson (English Puritan c.

1620 – 1686).”

And he concludes: “If we glorify God, he will glorify our souls forever. By raising God's glory, we increase our own: by glorifying God, we come at last to the blessed enjoyment of him.”

. . . .

EntreWorship Challenge:

Are you willing to let your imagination

fly beyond the stars, and allow yourself

to explore to the very edge of grace

to seek God's will and the

good works he planned for you?

. . . .

Embracing Prayer

A Conversation with Leslie Bianco

One of the first emails I read every day is from *In the Company of Prayer*, a daily prayer and brief reflection from a business leader or business book.

Leslie Bianco curates those prayers and reflections, publishing her *Morning Briefings* as an email service which reaches the global business community.

As a long-time subscriber myself, I was drawn to Leslie's purpose for *Company of Prayer*: "We're here to guide each other that one step further along a personal journey."

How do we guide one another if we're all following the same leader, the One who called us to life and to serve Him through our jobs and vocations? I think you know the answer; Leslie shared her perspective on how this happens:

2 Thessalonians 1:11 reads, "So we keep on praying for you, asking our God to enable you to live a life worthy of his calling. May he give you the power to accomplish all the good things your faith prompts you to do."

EW: Is The Company of Prayer is a business, a passion, a vocation, a ministry — or all of the above? How is Company of Prayer a response to a prompting of your faith?

Leslie: "In the Company of Prayer is a Delaware LLC currently operating from Seattle, WA. I started my career as a journalist, most notably as a staff writer and editor at *Bon Appetit* magazine. I left my 30th floor Wilshire Blvd world for my own scrappy start-up that I sold days after delivering my firstborn."

"In the ensuing years, I kept a toe in my profession, writing just about everything imaginable from home all the while immersing myself in my children's world through volunteer leadership roles. When my oldest was about to graduate high school, I was ready to formally reenter the business community using all those experiences, with my MBA as a jumping off."

"I remember pitching the idea to my entrepreneur husband, who was to be my emotional support and technology genius, and the one to help me front the expense; saying that I wasn't sure that it was the right time, financially, as a family to take this on. He responded, 'There's never really a good time, financially, to take on an endeavor such as this. You're either in it or you're not.'"

"I chose to serve the business community because these are my people. Not just from my own professional experiences but from the advantage of being a CEO's wife. I see clearly that this is a segment of society likely to be spiritually overlooked by the various faith communities. We are a start-up family, so I structured Company of Prayer as such, comfortable with all the rules of that particular entity, rather than a not-for-profit."

EW: What led you to start publishing the reflections, and why did you choose to focus on the business community?

Leslie: "The summer between the Y2K and September 11, I — or more specifically, my youngest daughter — received a postcard from the Vatican from her high school-age Sunday school teacher saying that she was praying for our family from there. That one postcard changed my life. In effect, she was saying, "I see you. I've had my eye on you. I'll continue to keep my eye on you. I value you." At the time, I was just so moved by the gesture, and so immature in my own faith development, that I really wasn't all that aware of what is now so obvious. That she was speaking on behalf of Christ. Our Morning Briefings focus on the businessperson's world. Their challenges, trials and triumphs are unique to their lifestyle."

2 Thessalonians continues: (1:12) Then the name of our Lord Jesus will be honored because of the way you live, and you will be honored along with him."

EW: How do you think what you do brings honor to Jesus?

Leslie: "Our entire "product" consists of a one sentence prayer, followed by three sentences of reflective content, delivered via email and social media. The idea is to get professionals, perhaps before they do anything else, to stop and collect themselves in community with others over the notion that they are prayerful people. For some people, it's baby steps, for now. Ultimately, these little pieces of content can lead them to deep and exacting insight and contemplation. Then we get out of the way and let the Almighty work His magic."

EW: How has the business community responded to you and Company of Prayer? Would you mind sharing a story from your readers of how your work has impacted them?

Leslie: "When I started out, I wanted to be that messenger; the one to say, "I see you. I've had my eye on you. I'll continue to keep my eye on you. I value you." But what "I've found is that those same Morning Briefing messages are being used as tools for the subscribers — who were originally intended to be the recipients of the messages — to become the givers of them. They do this, they tell me, by forwarding them on to the one person who most needs to hear it — an employee, customer, shareholder, vendor, family member. It's becomes a tool for healing, understanding, conversation."

EW: Do you have a board or mentors with whom you work? How do you decide what to publish?

Leslie: "I only have one Boss, and He controls the message. Of this, I am certain, as there are times when I publish something and I think, even I don't know what that's supposed to mean. Invariable, I get emails back, with subscribers telling me how spot-on it was for their particular circumstances that day. I am very protective of those messages. I guard them closely. I don't tell our readers what I think or how to think. I just say think. Pray. That very intentional responsibility is hard to articulate, and I guess I'm just not willing to share it, so, but for my husband, I go it alone, knowing that such a decision has likely stalled my growth."

EW: How do you personally approach your work as worship?
Leslie: "My work is a gift from God to me. I get to do this incredible thing. I get to gather, each morning, two or more of us, to a place where He can say, "I see you. I've had my eye on you. I'll continue to keep my eye on you. I value you." As I have furthered my own faith, I have had this incredible community to share it with."

Sign up for "Morning Briefings," and discover how prayer can be an inspirational and strategic tool in the management of your professional lives at companyofprayer.com.

Follow twitter.com/companyofprayer.

Read the article that explores the difference between your purpose and mission, with an example from In the Company of Prayer at aespire.com/blog/communications/ the-difference-between-your-purpose-and-mission.

No Looking Back

A Conversation with John Beckett

In Matthew 9 Jesus asks those with whom he is traveling to follow him. In the last verse, Jesus said "Anyone who puts a hand to the plow and then looks back is not fit for the Kingdom of God."

There is a cost to following Christ. The cost to you and me is the surrender of our will to his will; the cost to him was his life.

If your calling is to a career in business, you can't look back. To follow means to keep your eye on the one whom you're following, not the path behind you.

John Beckett was called to business at a young age, but he first realized it is his second calling.

2 Thessalonians 1:11 reads, "So we keep on praying for you, asking our God to enable you to live a life worthy of his calling. May he give you the power to accomplish all the good things your faith prompts you to do."

EW: In what way has your business career been a response to a prompting of your faith and calling?

John: "When I think of calling, I think of a statement by Os Guinness in his book, "The Call." He said our primary call is always to Christ — then to vocation."

"My call to Christ grew out of business challenges — the sudden death of my dad (our company's founder) and a devastating fire. At one point I realized I was on a fool's errand — trying to build a business in my own strength. Following my conversion, my call to vocation was confirmed when I sensed the Lord speak to me: 'John, I've called you to business. Do it with all your heart.'"

"That was five decades ago and I haven't looked back. My goal is indeed to live a life worthy of my dual callings — to the Lord and to business — and to do so with my fullest energy and capacities."

2 Thessalonians continues: (1:12) Then the name of our Lord Jesus will be honored because of the way you live, and you will be honored along with him."

EW: Loving Monday and Mastering Monday have made an impact on the lives of many business professionals and entrepreneurs. How has your writing brought honor to Jesus?

John: "My books were written out of a heart cry to help others in two specific ways: to live integrated lives where Mondays are of as great a value as Sundays, and secondly, to see biblical leaders like Joseph, Moses, Daniel, Lydia, David and even the Lord himself as highly capable workplace practitioners — folks whose examples we can profitably emulate."

"Grasping these two realities is truly liberating! Why, you or I can be an "ordained plumber!" I've found among those who have drawn from our experiences and applied them in their own spheres of influence, they've been helped on their journeys, and the Lord has been glorified."

EW: How do you serve the business community and your company's employees with love?

John: "In 1 Corinthians 13, the great passage on love, we may be surprised to learn the Apostle Paul says as much about what love is not, as what it is."

"That's a lesson for us — what to avoid as well as what to embrace. We show love to others when we avoid arrogance, self-centeredness, greed, indifference and passing judgment."

"True Christianity is found in humility, genuine caring, generosity and deep respect. These qualities touch hearts, which is where we engage others in effective and enduring ways."

EW: How do you personally approach your work as worship, and how are your business endeavors an expression of worship?

John: "'Work' and 'worship' derive from the same Hebrew root, 'avodah.' It's fascinating that they are related. How does this play out?"

"In true worship, we abandon ourselves to the Lord. In our work, we can give our all — to producing quality parts, making good decisions, solving knotty problems. "

"In worship, we express our adoration and affection. In or work, we are grateful for opportunities and challenges that enable us to honor God through our diligence and service."

"Worship is surrender. That's not a common term in our work — we want to win! — but just as we increase when we decrease (John 3:30), we prosper when we serve, always yielding to God's wisdom and sovereignty."

Q: What advice would you give to an entrepreneur who wants their faith to impact their work?

John: "The entrepreneur isn't the wild west gunslinger, as often portrayed. Rather he or she works carefully with limited resources, taking measured risks and working diligently to fulfill a dream."

"The greatest risk for the believing entrepreneur is going it alone — absent the wisdom, guidance and provision of God. In contrast, a sound approach is summarized in Proverbs 3:5: 'Trust in the Lord with all your heart and lean not on your own understanding.'"

"Faith isn't an add-on to work. Faith is the mainspring, the means by which everything else functions and has meaning."

Find more hope and inspiration for your
journey of work and faith at

EntreWorship.com
fb.com/EntreWorship
twitter.com/entreworship
instagram.com/entreworship

Brian Sooy is a design consultant, author, and principal of the marketing agency Aespire (aespire.com).

The stories and reflections from the journal of *EntreWorship*® are drawn from Brian's 30+ years of experience as an entrepreneur, business leader, and strategic advisor.

As the principal of Aespire he serves business, nonprofit, and ministry leaders who seek clarity and solutions to communications challenges.

Learn more about Brian's writing and design leadership at briansooy.com.

Other Books from Brian Sooy:

Raise Your Voice: A Cause Manifesto
ISBN-13: 978-1605440293

Raise Your Voice is an Amazon.com top-rated branding and marketing book for mission-driven organizations.

EntreWorship
ISBN 13: 978-1546460350

Children's Book Series

Luckey Haskins and the Zoo Adventure
ISBN-13: 978-1535283304

For the discriminating:
Typography:
Univers (Headlines and subtitles)
Chaparral Pro (Body copy and quotes)

Aespire follows Bringhurst's *Elements of Typographic Style*.

This book was printed by robots the day you ordered it.

The silky cover is a soft-touch matte laminate.
Feels good, doesn't it?